Existmankind
2022

Stephen W. Sweigart

ISBN 978-1-959895-53-4 (paperback)
ISBN 978-1-959895-65-7 (hardback)
ISBN 978-1-959895-52-7 (ebook)

Printed in the United States of America

WEST POINT
PRINT AND MEDIA

THE CREATION OF MANKIND

AND WOMENKIND

THE EXISTANCE OF THE UNIVERSE.

Who created god? Where did he come from?
If he or she is infinite, how is that possible?
God had to come from somewhere!
God may not be a creature like humans,
If infinite, and spiritual. Yet he had to
Come into existence. How did this god
Come into existence? You say, always was!
Yet the science theories of creation
Happened without a infinite cause!
I will explore in this poem.
Also, world mythologies of creation.

Einstein believed because of the cosmology
        of his day that the universe
                was eternal and unchanging.
Common knowledge had it this way.
        Friedmann, a Russian scientist, In 1922.
Began with the same belief
        that the universe had uniform density.
He reasoned that its geometry must not
        be fixed and unchanging with time.
          He became confident

It was therefore, that our universe must expand
and contract.
In history of science theoretical arguments
mathematic reasoning
have solved few debates.
Observations and data more often have.
In the 20th Century it was thought
that the Milky Way,
our galaxy, was the universe.
At first, they viewed
but could not decide whether
nearby clouds of gas,
these nebulae were galaxies.
In 1908, **Henrietta Leavitt**, an American,
discover a technique by which
certain pulsating stars,
identified as **Cepheids**,
were a unfailing source of how often
they emit pulses of light
and how bright these pulses were.
At this same time, telescopes were becoming
more powerful!
In 1919, with the **Hooker** telescope,
the biggest in world then.
Edwin Hubble measured the distance
of nebulae, so that they revealed

to be to remote,
to be part of our galaxy.
He observed that the **Andromeda Nebulae**
was in fact a galaxy.
Our galaxy, the Milky Way
was one of many in a greater universe.

The astronomer, **Vesto Slipher**,
was able to measure light
from galaxies, and how fast it is moving.
He realized that the light often
shifted toward lower frequencies,
or *redshifted*, moving away.

Hubble and **Milton Humason**,
made an impressive catalogue
of distances for forty-six galaxies.
Most were moving away from us
at substantial velocities.
The velocities of these galaxies
were proportionate
to their distance from us.
{**Hubble's Law**}
Yet we can also think of the universe
of expanding space as shrinking, besides increasing.
EVERYTHING! That is: Everything.

Hubble's discoveries told
about the past, also.
Out of a hot primordial state,
over a billion years.
Later, known as the '**Big Bang**'.

The universe from a very hot,
dense state over a period
of almost 14 billion years,
creating nuclei, atoms, galaxies, stars, and planets.
The data supporting this theory
Is overwhelming that no serious
scientist doubts this evidence.

The finding, by **Hubble**, that galaxies
are moving in velocities away
proportionate to their distance
is evidence that the universe
Is expanding and evolving in time.
That the universe is not perpetual or eternal.

In 1931, **Georges Lemaltre**, paper
'The beginning of the world
from the point of
View of **Quantum Theory**'.

Each particle of matter and photon of light
evolved from
the decay of a single 'atom'.
A truly gigantic mass equal
to the total energy of everything
in universe currently.
Before this sole primordial 'bit' decayed
the notions of space and time
had no meaning.
The essence of the 'Big Bang' theory.

As the expansion of space in time,
matter and energy within it
slowly diminishes.
A higher density of matter
was encompassed in our universe
in the past.
It will become even less so in future.
It is cooler now, then in hot past.
Everything was nearer together,
and the relative quantity of matter,
and other kinds of energy,
altered as this expansion took place.
Expansion of space and cosmological redshift
have reduced matter and light.

Our universe commenced in a state of Light.

Today there is more energy
        In the form of matter.

In the late 1950's, the theory
        of **stellar nucleosynthesis**,
the fusion of hydrogen into helium nuclei,
        could not produce the quantity
            of helium in our universe.

These nuclei formed a mixture
        of these two processes.
The lighter species of the periodic table
        generate in first few minutes
            of universal history.

In the **primordial Era**, there was extreme
            light and heat.
    It became evident that helium
            and other nuclear species
        was at hand at the '**Big Bang**'.
    The amount depended on
    how many protons were present?
These primordial protons have never
            disappeared.

In compared to the cold and large empty state
of our universe today.
Yet cosmic radiation is present everywhere.
Even today.
Nowhere was there emptiness.
All space was filled with light and heat.

As our universe expands, it continually cools.

During the first hundred years
after the '**Big Bang**',
all space was filled with protons,
electrons, and small groups
of protons, and neutrons
bound together as nuclei.
The chunks to create atoms existed,
but no '**atoms**' were present.
As the universe cooled, the electrons
bound themselves to protons
and helium nuclei,
producing complete '**atoms**'.

This a crucial event in cosmic history.
Our telescopes can only discern
light that originated after

this crucial event.
The blinding of electrons
and protons filled **plasma**.
This opaque plasma altered
into gas of electrically
neutral hydrogen and helium atoms.
The cold environment of cosmic radiation
can be challenging for scientist
to detect and study.

Arno Penzias and **Robert Wilson**,
two radio scientists,
turned the **Holmdel** telescope,
of New Jersey, into one that searches
for radio waves from astronomical sources,
all through the **Milky Way**.
As they searched the sky, they keep
Collecting continual hiss.
It was thought that it might be
protons traveling since
the first atoms formation.
Scientist continued to measure
the spectrum of this radiation
It became clear that the observed radiation
was the very cosmic environment
that were consistent with

that what was predicated
in the '**Big Bang**' theory.

In 1978, **Penzias** and **Wilson** were awarded
the **Noble Prize** in **Physics**.

Modern observations have raised questions.
Only about 15 percent of matter
comprising of protons, neutrons, and
atoms or molecules.
The other 85 percent is something unknown.
We name '**dark matter**'.
In the 1990's it became evident that
our universe has been expanding
faster and faster.
Despite past beliefs that was slowing.
A massive amount of energy force is required.
More than all that is possible in
our universe matters.
We name this energy '**dark energy**'.

In the first moments after the 'Big **Bang**',
all of space was energetic elements
making a dense soup.
These quantum particles can be
be created and destroyed spontaneously.

More can be learned about them with tools,
like **'particle accelerates'**.

What is a **particle accelerator**?
Is a device that accelerates
elementary particles, such as
electrons or protons,
to very high energies.
There are two kinds of particle accelerates.
Linear and circular.
Linear thrust particles
along a straight or fixed beam line,
for fixed target experiments.
Circular accelerates particles
around a circular track, used
for colliding beams or fixed
experiments.
They speed up and increase
energy of a beam of particles
with electrical fields.
The beam of particles
travel inside a vacuum in a metal
beam pipe.
Particles must travel unhindered
in a dust and air free environment.

Electromagnets handle and aim
        as they travel.
      Electric fields switch from positive
          to negative at given sequences
creating radio waves that accelerate
      particles in clusters.
They can be guided to fixed targets
          or to two beams that can collide.
      Detectors record and reveal
        radiation and particles
that are produced by collisions
      between them and targets.
The accelerators are essential in discovery
        for **Particle Physics**, or
      Energy Physics, so they can
achieve understanding of Fundamental's
        practical and physical laws
that rule matter, energy, space and time.

Andrei Sakharov, a Soviet scientist, who first
               was involved
       in Soviet nuclear weapon program.
He realized the great danger of these weapons.

He became aware of its great dangers,
        and directed his activities

to peaceful ventures.
He reinvented himself as a particle physicist
and cosmologist.
He respected the **symmetry**
between matter and antimatter,
as other particle physicist.
Yet as a cosmologist he knew that
our universe had *transitioned*
into a state where there was *more*
matter, then antimatter.
Sakharov in a paper explained how
this **transition** took place in 1967.

Three conditions:
1. Baryon number violation.
2. C-symmetry and CP-symmetry violations.
3. Interactions out of thermal equilibrium.

Baryons are subatomic particles, such as
a nucleon or hyperon, that has a mass
equal to or greater than that of a proton.

Protons are a stable subatomic particle occurring
in all atomic nuclei, with a positive electric
charge equal in magnitude to that of an
electron, but of opposite sign.

Electrons are subatomic particles with a charge
   of negative electricity in solids.
Nucleus is the positivity.
Neutrons are a subatomic particle of about
   the same mass as a proton but without
   an electric charge, present in an atomic
   nuclei except those of ordinary hydrogen.

The **first** situation is to convert a world
   that it contains an equal number of quarks
   and anti-quarks, into one with only quarks.
   An interaction that creates a net number
   of quarks or destroying net anti quarks.

Quarks are any number of subatomic particles
   carrying a fractional electric charge,
   postulating as building blocks of the
   hadrons. Quarks have not been directly
   observed but theoretical predictions
   based on existence have been confirmed
   experientially.

Hadrons is a composite subatomic particle
   made of two or more quarks held together
   by the strong interaction.

The **second** situation, **C-symmetry** is an abbreviation
of the phase '**charge configuration symmetry**',
used physical laws under charge. **CP symmetry**
is that the laws of physics should be the same
if a particle is interchanged with its antiparticle
as its spatial organizes are inverted. **CP violation**
(**C**) **charge** configuration (**P**) **parity** by the weak
force, which is responsible for the radioactive
decay of atomic nuclei.
Matter cancels out antimatter, rather than
canceling out each other. There must be a law
in Nature which prefers matter and is bias
against antimatter.

Symmetry in physics is when a little is done to it,
it will leave it unchanged.
Symmetries are the spirit of modern Physics.
Few are as important as that of parity, charge
and time.
Parity symmetry is that of space. In which
that of a wave function representing
a system of fundamental particles.

Parity is the state of being equal. In mathematics
the fact of being even or odd.

Charge symmetry is that the interchange
of opposite members of a multiples of subatomic
particles in a system or process that
does not affect any property of the system
or outcome of the process.
Time symmetry is if moving forward does not
distinguish from moving backwards in time.

Time symmetry implies that the laws of physics
look the same when time runs
Forward or backwards.
That does not hold true
for all physical interactions.

The **third** situation, in which all parts are of equal
temperature is interacted rapidly or violently not
in that state.

BIG BANG:

The earliest time period is when very small
dense, and hot and it cooled down
when the universe expanded.
The expansion is called **inflation**
by cosmologist.

It became filled with an equal amount
of matter and anti-matter
in which matter was more in quality.
Latter combined with other particles
to form matter all over.
Then after one second it became more
and more expanded and cooled.
It is a world which one can exist.
After 100 seconds
of the temperature cooled
to 1 billon degree Kelvin.
The subatomic particles continually
combined with each other.
Except electrons which collided
with other particles to form.
At 56,000 years it cooled
9000 degrees Kelvin.
Resulting into a density of matter
allocation to meet
the density radiation.
After 324,000 years it cooled down
to 3,000 degrees Kevin,
and electrons and protons
come together to form
different hydrogen atoms.
The first moment when the universe formed,

after 380,000 years
cosmic microwave backward radiation locked away.
After a 100 million more years to expand
and cool along with gravitational
fluctuation nonstop to allow particles
of matter to cluster and combine.
Then stars were created when gases break down
due to the conduct of gravity
which it made denser and hotter.
The stars combine to create galaxies
and *supernova*.
The eruption of the stars gave birth
to matter which spewed out
in the universe and
created our solar system
4.6 billion years ago.

DARK MATTER

Is a nonluminous material that is hypothesized
to exist in space and that could
take any of several forms.
Including weakly interacting particles
(**cold** dark matter)

or high-energy randomly moving particles
formed soon after the Big Bang.
(**hot** dark matter)
In some cosmological theories.

It is discerned from it's gravitational attraction
rather than it's luminosity.
It makes up 30.1 percent of the energy-composition
of the universe, dark energy 69.4, and
visible matter .05 percent.

BLACK HOLE

The smallest black holes formed
when the universe begun.
They are as small as atoms. Their mass
Or matter is as much as a mountain.
Black holes that are created when star fall
On itself or collapses.
Are called a **supernova**,
An exploding star that blast
A part into space.
Made same time as their galaxy.
The **supermassive** are more than one million
Suns together. Every galaxy has a **supermassive.**

A **Black hole** in the center.
The **Milky Way** has one **'Sagittarius A'**
It has a mass of 4 million suns.

In one theory, **time** has *existed forever*.
Yet unlike the static models of the past,
The universe alters as *eons* go on.
In another scheme, **time**, *did not exist*
Before the **'Big Bang'**.
Time arises out of nothing, a **Planck**, a tiny
Finite size. It expands thereafter.
There was no moment prior to the smallest size,
Since there was no prior, no creation
Of the universe. It was neither created or
Destroyed, it **'BE'**. It exists without **time**.

The **'Planck'** is the smallest size
we can divide space.
Some physicists have proposed
That bodies are far smaller than quarks,
Called **'strings'** they are not *point*
Particles like electrons, they are
A **'string'** of energy.
They occupy a space nine or ten

Dimensions, instead of three.
If they really exist it is known that
space and time lose their significance
At '**Planck**' size.

If the universe has a **twin** and on that twin
It runs *backwards* then dark matter
could be explained.
Prior to the '**Big Bang**'
. an **anti-universe**
could be running backwards.
A new theory states that *'dark matter'*
is a new variant of a particle
called '**neutrino**'.
Expanding '**Inflation**'
would not be necessary.
Future experiments in the search for
for gravitational waves or to
find neutrinos could prove
if mirror image of universe exists.

A new theory if **symmetry** is important
that applies
to the entire universe itself.

This extends from just force and fields
to the entire psychical object
of the universe.
The universe is expanding
it is filled with particles
evolving
moving forward in time.
To conserve the **CPT symmetry**
all over the cosmos
there must be a *mirror-image* cosmos
that balances out our own.
It would have opposite charges
than ours, a mirror
and run backward in time.
Obeying **CPT symmetry**.
It would not need
for a swift expansion,
'inflation'.
Neutrinos would be In the blend.
There are three *types* of neutrinos
all which are spinning
to the left.
Yet the corresponding universe would
call for at least one
right spinning neutrino.
They would be largely invisible,

only influencing the rest
of the universe through gravity.
It would be a lot like dark matter
filling only with gravity sounds.
Enough right spinning neutrinos.
to account for dark matter.

Never having an entry to this mirror image
because it exists behind the '**Big Bang**',
before the beginning of time.
But it can be tested.
Can be foreseen that the three-left spinning
neutrino species are
'**Majorana**' particles
and that they are their own
antiparticles.
One of the neutrinos
should be massless.
In this model the universe
is filled with particles
naturally of its own.
There are no gravitational waves,
unlike with '**inflation**'.

Mythological creation

There are 5 types of Creation Myths

1.   From Chaos
2.   Ex Nihilo
3.   Dismemberment of Being
4.   Pure Being from Deity
5.   Earth Diver

Heliopolis --- Egyptian

Nun, the primeval ocean. At its center was
Benben, a giant pyramid. **Atum**, the creator deity,
arose. **Atum** was the incarnation of the Sun.
     Life came forth in an asexual existence.
The first deities were created:

Shu, air. **Tefnut**, moisture, or water.
The forces of chaos were kept in balance.
Atum's goddess **Ma'at**, truth and order, helped him.
Shu and **Tefnut** brought forth **Geb**, earth and
Nut, sky. They were inseparable.
Yet **Atum** instructed **Shu** to separate them.
They gave birth before separation to the deities:
Osiris, **Isis**, **Seth**, and **Nephthys**.
The Egyptians of *Memphis,* the god **Ptah**,
The god of craft and architecture,
Was the major deity, believed to envision
The universe and as he imaged,
And materialized into existence.

Early Indo-European

Ymir, a power that existed before time.
A vast sea of chaos, **Ginnungagap**.
Devoid of life, structure or order.
Sucked on the primitive cow, **Audhumia**.
From **Ymir's** perspirations came forth
two gigantic giants. A third then
appeared.

Audhumia nurtured on salt residues,
 named **Buri**.
Audhumia creamed **Buri**, and the chains
 that held him waned. His son, **Borr**
 went on to marry **Ymir**,
 giving birth to **Bestla**.
After **Borr** and **Bestla** mated **Odin**,
the all-father gods, in Norse mythology,
 came to life.
Odin, envious of his grandfather, **Ymir**,
 killed him, dismembering his body
 forming the world, we know.
From the flesh came the Earth.
From his sweat the oceans and seas.
From the bones, mountains.
From his hair trees and plants.
From his skull erupted the sky.
From his brains the clouds.
 Midgard, the Earth came from
the eyebrows of **Ymir**, used to
create the first humans: **Ask** and **Embla**.

Finnish creation

There was only sky and primal waters.
  Ilmatar, the daughter of the sky,
She dove into the waters to rest.
  Swimming for 700 years
She discovered a colorful bird,
  Looking for land,
She allowed it to it to land on her.
She laid six golden eggs
  And one iron on her knee.
The egg fell and cracked,
The shells created land,
The whites' stars and moon.
The yoke the sun.

Mayan creation

In the *Book of the Community* '**Popul Vuh**'

In the beginning of time was nothingness,
  devoid of structure or order.
Teoeu, the maker, and **Gucumatz**,

the feathered spirit.
Joined their thoughts to create the universe.
They created '**man**'. First out of clay,
which failed. Then wood,
also failing, then out of maize dough.
Succeeding which was able
to speak, feel, and think.
The Sun, Moon, and Stars were created
a place for their creation, **Earth**.
Four kinds of creatures were formed.
A parrot, coyote, fox, and crow.
Because they could not speak,
they became subservient to '**human beings**'.

Babylonian creation

In the beginning their were two gods:
Abzu and **Tiamat**.
Abzu was god of chaos or ocean,
Tiamat the god of fresh water.
They gave birth to new gods.
Tiamat hated the new gods, and
set out to obliterate them.
The new gods discovered his hate,

and threw a net over him, beating him.
His body created the sky, while
the rest, human beings, animals,
plants, and other creatures.

Ancient Greek creation

The **Titan**, **Prometheus**, created *man*.
In the beginning the universe
was an endlessness, **Nyx**,
the deity of darkness.
Nyx laid an egg, laying for years,
then emerging. Producing **Eros**
the deity of *Love*.
The broken shells became sky and earth.
Gaia, was the earth. Known as a goddess.
Uranus, the sky. They mated bringing forth
The **Titans: Hekatonkheires, Cyclopes**,
Oceanus, Crius, Iapetus, Tethys,
Phoebe, and **Korunas**.
Korunas overthrew **Uranus**, and with **Rhea**,
Another generation of gods: **Zeus, Hera,**
Hades, Poseidon, Hestia, and **Demeter.**

Zeus, the King of **Olympus**, overthrew
   Korunas.
After the battle of the **Titans**, **Zeus** allowed
   Prometheus to create humans
   out of clay. His brother, **Epimetheus**,
   created animals.
Prometheus valued mankind more than **Zeus**
   he stole **FIRE** from heaven, and bequiffed
   to mankind. **Zeus** bound **Prometheus**
   to a rock, in which an eagle pecked
   on his liver. Freed years later by **Hercules**.

Ainu creation

The creation myth of **Japan**, emerged
   from the **Ainu** people.
It was broken into three sections.
   '**mosir noskekehe**' the world's center.
'Mosir **sikah ohta**' a time when
   the universe was born.
'**mosir kes**' the end of the world.

The creator god dispatched his trusted
   water wagtail to create land
   from cosmic ocean.

The bird separated it with its wings
to one side, creating islands.
They populated these islands.

Maori **creation**

The **Maori** culture of the Pacific Islands,
Rangi and **Papa**, the Earth and Sky deities
Were locked up in eternal embrace.
Giving birth to males who were in darkness
And nothingness. They desired light, the gods
Separated them, creating a space
For the universe.

Native American creation

In the many native American cultures.
        The **raven** is the strongest
                creature in the cosmos.
Many tribes regarded the raven
        the creator of the universe.
In one myth the **raven** came across
        a full-grown adult man who

he approached to inquire about
  where he appeared from.
The man responded that he lived in
  the inside of a *pea pod*
for four days, and on fifth came out
  a full-grown person.
The man told the raven that he employed
  the water in the pod, to relieve
  the pain in his abdomen.
The **raven** thought they were similar
  and implored him to wait.
  While he gathered berries.
The **raven** ordered him to eat the berries.
  He took man to a creek,
  The raven tapped four objects,
    Bringing them to life.

The **Iroquois** myth a female deity fell
  from the heavens, and the otter, duck,
beaver, and muskrat dove in the water
    creating an island, out of mud.
In the **Seneca** the chief's daughter exacted
  with a serious illness. The only cure
    was to lay besides a tree, revealed
  in a dream, and have it burrowed up.
A man complained that the tree was his

his whole income. He kicked
her through the opening. She fell from
heavens and was rescued by a waterfowl.
A turtle offers to take her to a new dwelling
place, and a toad dives in to the sea, and
              carries soil onto the turtles back,
         forming land.
The **Wyandot**, is very similar.
The **Hopi** culture is a cyclical creation
         Now in the fourth. Each version
The people began happy and kind.
         Then they became disobedient
              And reckless, not in peace.
The *spider woman* mid-wife, Earth mother,
         Would lead honorable to the next universe.
The **Zuni** culture the fifth world
         is the '**Daylight World**'.
Where we now exist. In the fourth
         A secret underground in darkness.
Near the center of Earth, they began.
With assistance of Deities, they created
Prayer sticks, and climbed to the fifth world.
Cherokee creation had only sky and sea.
         The *water beetle* who dwelled in the sky
         Wanted to know what was below the sea.
         He dove in, after swimming,

He desired to rest, at the bottom
He bought up mud, building
An island.

Zoroastrian creation

Its faith states there was two opposites
deities in the beginning of time:
Ahura Mazda and **Angra Mainya**.
The deities of light and darkness.

Ahura Mazda created angels/beings.
Who helped him spread light
across the universe.
Amesha Spentas *'Holy Immortals'*
with his archangels divide
the universe into two sections:
the spiritual and physical.
The physical section was created
3,000 years after the spiritual.
The perfect man and bull were
then created.
Angra Mainya created all the evils,

and demons, that were to encounter
Ahura Mazda's creations. Also
creating snakes, flies, ants,
mosquitoes, spiders and others.
They produced pain, diseases, and death.
Perfect man and bull gave way to the evils,
over time. From **perfect** man's body,
first man and woman came forth.
Mashya and **Mashynag**. From the bull
came forth trees, and vegetation.

Sumerian creation – Eridu Genesis

Unearthed in modern *Afak*, **Iraq**, the **Nippur**,
described the main deities, **An**, the sky father,
Enlil, the earth and wind, **Enki**, water,
knowledge, and mischief, and **Ninhursanga**,
mother goddess.
They created the world, as well as human beings
to populate it.

The gods decided that mankind was not of value
saving from a enormous flood. Yet **Enki**, the god
of water, alerted mankind and instructed him
to build an Ark, that could save humanity from

the torrential rain, that lasted for seven days
and nights.

Another myth says the builder of the Ark
was not, **Atrahsis**, but **Ziusudra**, the ruler of
Shuruppak.
Once the floods end, the sun God, **Utu**,
appears out of the window of the Ark.
Ziusudra, bows down before **Uru**.

Buddhist creation

There is no creation myths in **Buddhism,**
But there is beliefs about creation.
Pangu's breath turned into wind and clouds.
His *eyes* became sun and moon.
Limbs and head turned into mountains.
His muscle Into fertile land.
His hair became the stars and galaxies.
His voice transformed into thunder.
The parasites that feast on his body
The first human beings.
Pangu In most myths emerged from an egg.

Hindu creation

Birth, death, and rebirth is essential.
In one myth, in the beginning there was
a mighty **Cobra**, that lived in a enormous
cosmic ocean. In the hands of the **Cobra**
lay the sleeping **Vishnu**, the creator god.
A **lotus** after time arose from **Vishnu**
navel. Within the **lotus** another god
of creation, **Brahma** or **Svayambhu**.
The lord of speech, **Brahma**, conceived
the idea of creating the universe.
He went into a significant state of meditation
For several *eons*, in order to do so.
Brahma, the four headed god, divided
the **lotus** into three sections, heavens, sky,
and earth. Animals and plants were gifted
the earth in all forms and sizes. The first humans
were also created to habitat the earth.
Shiva is the god of rebirth, and destruction,
comprising of the triumvirate gods, that make
up birth, death, and rebirth.
In another myth **Hiranyagarbha**,
the Golden Womb floats through primordial
Chaos between incarnations of the universe.

Genesis creation –
Hebrew, Christian, Islam.

The supreme being was hovering over the vast
cosmic water. He created the world in six days,
and on the seventh rested.

On day **one**, he commanded light to come forth
then separated light from darkness.

On the **second** day, **God** separated sky from
the waters. Collecting the waters into one place,
becoming the sea.

On the **third** day, created vegetation on the dry
land.

On the **fourth** day, **God** created the Sun, Moon,
and Stars, in the cosmos.

On the **fifth** day, **God** created after being pleased
with his progress, the sea and land animals.

On the **sixth** day, **God** created the first man,
Adam, in his own image. From Adam's rib came
forth the first woman, **Eve**, to serve as Adam's
companion.

The first human beings were placed in a
marvelous garden, **Eden**. In that paradise like
condition, they experienced no suffering, death,
Or unhappiness.
In **Eden** was the **tree of knowledge**, in which
they were not permitted to eat. A serpent
convinced them that it was good to eat from it.
They were cast out of the garden, **Eden**, by **God**,
for their disobedience. As were their
descendants, to live in pain, sickness, and death.

Yoruba creation – The golden chain

This myth comes from West Africa, mostly **Nigeria**,
In the beginning the gods lived in happiness
the sky. **Olorun**, the king of the gods, and the queen
Olokun. They lived in bliss, but the lesser god known
As **Obatala**, was not satisfied. He desired to have
other beings besides celestial. He conferred in,
Olurun's oldest son, and he told him to make golden
chain. He filled it with snail shells, palm nuts,
a black cat, and a white hen.
Obatala stooped from the sky, with his magical
chain. He created the land and all creatures.

He placed the substances of the chain in a pit, and
brewed wine from palm fruit and became drunk
and created human beings, which were fallible
because he was intoxicated.
The **Kuba** culture from central Africa.
There was darkness and water occupied
By a giant, **Mbombo**, in pain he vomited up
The sun, moon and stars into existence.
The sun evaporated the water creating
The clouds and land. He felt better,
Yet again fell ill and created the animals.

Chinese creation

The universe began as a chaotic soup
        without any shape.
A black **egg** lay in this universe which
        contained a gargantuan creature.
        A hairy giant with two horns and two tusks.
Known as **Pangu**, he is alleged to have slept
        In the egg for more than 18,000 years.
        During his sleeping the universe was kept
        in perfect balance.

Yiu, darkness; **Yan**, light.
Upon waking, he proceeded to escape
      from shell of egg.
    Therefore, shattering perfect balance.
yang, the top half of shell, became the sky.
yin, the bottom half, the earth.
    As he pressed up he grew taller, ten feet.
Aiding in task, were **Qulin**, **Phoenix**,
    the **Dragon**, and the **Turtle**.
For 18,000 years he would do, before dying.
    His body fell to the earth, transforming
      Into the earth.
Breath, wind and clouds. Eyes, sun and moon.
Members and head, mountain. Muscles, fertile land.
Facial hairs, stars and galaxy. Voice, thunder.
From the parasites that feed on his body, **humans**.

315,000 years ago, or so.
    Human **evolution**, the means
By which human beings developed
    On Earth from non-extinct primates.
We are **Homo sapiens**, viewed zoologically.

A culture-bearing upright walking species.
That inhabits the land.
Most likely evolved first in Africa.

Human beings and **apes** developed
Separately.
The fossils found so far indicate
That they vary in past as they do now.

Biological creation

Anaximander of Miletus, a Greek philosopher
Lived in the 500's B.C.E. He believed
That life began in the sea.
Our ancestors must be fish, since their
Young immediately begin living.
Our children are born needing to be nurtured.
He was correct human ancestry can be traced
To the sea and fish.

Charles Darwin published his
'On the Origins of Species'
Along with his contemporary

Alfred Russell Wallace
They termed '**natural selection**'.
Sometimes called '**survival of fittest**'.
Those organisms that are physically
Fit to survive grow to maturity and reproduce.
The others never reach that age, or
Reproduce as much.
There are those that are best suited to their
environment, and most likely
To pass their qualities on to the next generation.
If the environment changes the qualities
That enhance survival also adopt.
'**Genetic drift**' is that certain organisms
by chance reproduce more
Because their genes get passed on.
They may not be fittest.

Different living organisms evolve
from earlier forms.

Evolution by natural selection
was first *demonstrated* by observation
that more offspring are often
Produced that can conceivably survive.
Attributes vary among individuals
With respect to their morphology,

Psychology and behavior
(*phenotypic variation*).
Distinct attributes confer different
Levels of survival and reproduction
(differential fitness).
Attributes can be passed from
generation to generation
(*heritability of fitness*).
Their survival is also dependent
On their individual environment.

(LUCA) last universal common ancestor.
Everyone creature shares inhabited
From 3.5 to 3.8 million years ago.
Fossil records document patterns
Of biodiversity that formed.
Mechanist biologist believe that
Living creatures
Are just atoms, and molecules.
Macroscopic winches and controls,
Chemicals and currents.
Vitalists believe there is a special quality
To life. Immaterial forces
That the Greeks called *'**pneuma**'*
Or **breath**.

The first creation of a complete set genes
From their chemical portions
And injections into large cells
Occurred in 2010.
They are trying to create life from non-life.

In 2003 a common mineral clay formed
from volcanic ash and used
In pet litter, it could step up
Cell parts for life.
It had already help assemble
RNA molecules
(essential in coding, etc. of genes).
Fatty acids also could bond
With clay to form membranes.
These assembled to form pouches.

That grew by themselves
When with other fatty acids were
Passed through a porous material
Would divide in a sense
like reproduction.

Ideas of *'Vitalism'*

In the eight century BC the royal Egyptian,
Kuttamuwa constructed
an eight-hundred-pound monument
to house his immortal soul.
In the eleventh century the Persian **Avicenna**.
Stated that since we think and are
Self-aware that even if we
Were disconnected totally from all
Sensory input, there
Must be a nonmaterial soul
In us.

It has been shown that '**urea**'
Has been synthesized from
An organic substance
From non-organic chemicals.
Also, that energy of food consumption
Is equal to energy in movement
respiration, and other activities.
As modern biologist demonstrated *'**non vitalism**'*.

Eternal intelligence

Intelligent life is in infinite future.
        Constant survival of intelligence
In the infinite future.
        Though all life will end
At some point in a hundred billion years!
The universe will continue in 'infinite time'.
        Life and the notion of 'biocentrism',
May go on after this cessation,
        In *intangible* forms!
Not as it has been known over the past,
        Since the first evolution of creatures.

The **Guth-Linde** theory was developed
        in the years 1979-1986.
It is a modification of the **Inflation theory.**

The Big Bang theory has limitations.

1. The **flatness** problem.
        It has been determined that the geometry
Of the universe is nearly flat. In Big Bang
        Cosmology curvature grow with time.

2.   The **Horizon** problem.
      Distant regions of space in opposite
directions of the sky are so far apart,
      Would never be in contact with each other.
The uniformity of microwave background
Tells us that they must have been contact in
past.
3.   The **Monopole** problem.
      A large number of heavy, stable
'**magnetic monopoles**' have never been
Observed, and if exist, will be much smaller
And rare.

The 'new' Inflation theory solves these problems:

The Flatness problem.
      Inflation stretches out any Initial curvature.
The Horizon peoblem.
      The inflation supposes a burst of expansion.
In the early universe it follows that the distant
      Regions were closer together originally.
The Monopole problem.
      Magnetic monopoles exist prior to Inflation.
      Then their density drops and their
      abundance become undetectable.

To have *Life* bodies one must not only
    Reproduce, but *evolve* through time.
Life on Earth, '*Earth Life*', consist
    Of four elements:
Hydrogen, oxygen, carbon, and nitrogen.
    All other elements comprise
Of less than one percent of mass
    Of living organisms.
These elements are of the six most
    Abundant in the universe.
Helium. and neon almost never comprise
    To develop into Life.
They are even more plentiful in Stars,
    And raise the possibilities of Life
Throughout the universe.

The epoch of missing geological period
    Also includes the period of *bombing*
Of craters and comets of the Earth.
    They consist of Life materials
That might have formed complex molecules.
    The origin of Life might have taken
    Millions of years.
It is also known that dinosaurs were made

Extinct from these collisions.
Geologist discovered enormous craters,
From this time period.

Evolutionary biology is now concerned
With the differences of creatures
And their DNA and RNA which
Reveal by its information
How to function and reproduce.
The '*evolutionary differences*' have been
Recorded in a '*tree of Life*'.
Its three limbs comprise of
Archaea, Bacteria, and Eucarya.
Eucarya is with cells that have nucleus
That are defined.
They have genetic material regulating
Its reproduction.
Archaea are 'extremophiles' life
That exist in extremes.
Temperatures near or above boiling
Point of water. High acidity, and
And other situations that would kill.
These are the oldest forms of life.

Oceanographers' submersible vehicles
　　Have discovered the first deep sea
　　　　Openings a mile and a half beneath
　　The Pacific Ocean, hottest
　　　　　And coolest on edges.
　　　　There live countless life forms.
Life near deep sea openings depends on
　　　'*chemosynthesis*' chemical reactions
　　Which hang on to geothermal heating.
As those that believe that life began in ponds
　　　　Or tide pools. High temperature
Origins of life, in which highly ordered
　　　　Structure of iron pyrite crystals
　　On whose surface the first complex
　　　　　Molecules might form.

Astrobiologist deal with life
　　　　beyond the earth.
They ponder about extraterrestrial life
　　　Or simulate these environments.

The $10 billion James Webb Space Telescope
Is seeing nearer to the dawn of time
And the edge of the universe,
By humanity more than ever before.
"What we saw to today is the early universe"
It is 1.5 million kilometers
Away from earth.
Scientist will be able to zoom 13.7 billion light years,
Nearer to the cosmic entities.
Even our solar system, with sharp focus.

www.ingramcontent.com/pod-product-compliance
Lightning Source LLC
Chambersburg PA
CBHW032104020426
42335CB00011B/477